Aging Gracefully

TIM CHALLIES

CRUCIFORM PRESS | JUNE 2018

CruciformPress
@CHALLIES

AUTHOR

Tim Challies is a Christian, a husband to Aileen, and a father to three teenage children. He is a co-founder of Cruciform Press and has written several books, including *Devoted*, *Visual Theology*, *Do More Better*, and *Sexual Detox*. He worships and serves as a pastor at Grace Fellowship Church in Toronto, Ontario and writes daily at www.challies.com.

 *We all know the feeling: every week, every month, every year it just seems that life keeps moving faster and faster. So we've taken our trademark length—books of about 100 pages—and added a set of resources that will make for even a quicker read. Cruciform Quick: a new line of booklets in the range of 40 to 60 pages each.*

AGING GRACEFULLY

Print / PDF ISBN: 978-1-941114-42-1
Mobipocket ISBN: 978-1-941114-43-8
ePub ISBN: 978-1-941114-44-5

Table of Contents

Building Our House

Every day, we are all building the house we will live in when old age comes. Some of us are building a beautiful palace. Some are building a dark prison. What are you building?

Perhaps you are building a house that will prove beautiful and comfortable through the long winter of your old age. You are decorating it tastefully, filling it with ornaments designed to bring pleasure and comfort in the days to come—deeds of gratitude and grace, acts of generosity and selfless love. On every wall, you are hanging pictures that are as meaningful as they are beautiful—warm friendships in Christ, mentoring and discipling relationships, children and grandchildren who know and love the Lord. These pictures look down upon you to comfort, to cheer, to encourage. You have stockpiled supplies of godliness and grace to ensure you will be full and fed, faithful in the days of weariness. You have gathered great stores of God's Word to fuel the fire, to keep it blazing brightly through the long winter days and nights. You have prepared a comfortable bed where you can lie and rest. As you draw your last breaths, you will be able to look from your bed to see those ornaments, those paintings, that lifetime of precious treasure, and you will know: you have lived a meaningful life.

Or perhaps you are building a house that will prove little more than a cold, gloomy prison through the long winter of your old age. You are decorating it with ugliness and kitsch— meaningless achievements, evil deeds, self-righteous works. You are covering the walls with grotesque pictures—harmful friendships, broken relationships, children and grandchildren who are wanton and rebellious. They look down upon you to haunt you, to condemn you, to fill you with fear and sorrow. You have stocked sparse supplies to feed upon in the days of weariness, leaving you to chew on bitterness, regret, and a thousand empty vices. You have gathered little of God's Word to fuel the fire, so it will burn low and extinguish, leaving you cold and miserable. You have prepared a bed of thorns where you will lie and desperately try to rest. As you draw your last breaths, you will look from your painful bed to see those awful ornaments, those dark paintings, that lifetime of piled regret, and you will know: you have wasted your life.[1]

Which house are you building?

Are you building a palace or a prison? Are you building a place of joy, comfort, and security, or a place of grief, sorrow, and peril? Every moment you are laying the bricks to your home. From childhood you have been decorating it. With each passing day you add new ornaments and you stock—or don't stock—it for days to come. And as the winter of your life approaches, you will take up residence in the house you have built.

So I ask again, which house are you building?

A DEEP FEAR, A DEEP LONGING

There are certain behaviors I have been conditioned to fear since childhood. I saw people act in certain ways, I saw the consequences of their actions, and I decided that I would never do those things. I decided I would not be like those people.

As a child I saw the abuse of alcohol. I saw full-out drunkenness in all its ugliness, all its shame. I saw it in people I loved, people in my extended family. I saw how they behaved, I saw how others treated them, I saw how their reputations crumbled. Even as a child and a teen, I found myself so wary of alcohol that it never was attractive to me. Even today I don't drink, and it's not because I have a biblical case against alcohol. It's that I'm just not interested. I never have been.

Since childhood, I have also been conditioned to fear aging poorly. I saw elderly people who behaved shamefully, who displayed so little of the dignity that ought to be associated with age. I saw old women who were embittered, who seemed to have no real point or purpose to their lives. I saw old men who were drunks, who were perverts, who were full of resentment toward God. Of course, I saw positive examples as well, dear old men and women who loved one another, who loved Jesus more than anything, who exemplified godliness and grace. Some of them I knew, and some I met in their books or their biographies. I developed a fear of aging poorly and a deep longing to age well.

When I was young, I resolved that I would age with grace. I would not be a dirty old man, an embittered old man, a drunken old man, a purposeless old man. I determined that in old age I would be dignified and godly, I would exemplify character and purposeful living to the end. Even then, I understood that this resolution would need to shape my entire life. I could not live a dissolute life and expect God to grant me the gift of godliness on my 65th birthday. I could not live an apathetic or lukewarm life and expect a purposeful, meaningful old age. If I wanted to be godly then, I'd need to learn to be godly now. If I wanted to live those days with purpose, I would first need to live these days with purpose. For these reasons and many more, the subject of aging is especially precious to me.

AGING AND OLD AGE

It is important to distinguish here between aging and old age. While old age is the position, aging is the process—the process of hard-fought, small investments made over time that determine our final position. My aim in this booklet is to bring attention to aging: the universal and lifelong reality that from the moment of birth we are growing older, that from our first breath we are progressing toward our last breath, that our every decision is culminating into the old man or old woman we'll be. Aging is the dash on the tombstone, the little line that in its progress from left to right, from the joy of birth to the sorrow of death, encapsulates a whole life. Aging comes with many sorrows and many joys, and in between them are the responsibilities we can choose to embrace or ignore.

I have written this with many tears—tears enough to surprise me and to show how deeply I feel this subject, how much it has been a track playing in the background of my life, how much it remains a deep desire. These are tears of sorrow for wasted opportunities, tears of joy for evidences of undeserved grace, tears of hope that God will grant my prayers. For there are few longings in my heart deeper than this: that God would let me live a godly, purposeful, dignified old age.

In this booklet, I aim to explore what the Bible says about aging. Ultimately, I want to encourage both you and me to age gracefully, to age wisely, to age resolutely to the glory of God.

CHAPTER 1

Greater Age Brings Greater Sorrow

Our only experience of aging is within this sinful world. We don't know what aging would have looked like if this world had remained unsullied by sin. We do know, however, that aging would have still occurred. Before God created people, God created time. So God created people to exist within time and pass through it. Thus, babies would have grown to be children, and children would have matured into adulthood. Perhaps the benefits that come with aging would have continued eternally without any of the negative effects we see and experience. We just don't know.

What we do know is that in a world like this one, aging has a strong association with pain and sorrow. Though aging is not without its benefits, it is known first for its sorrows. We experience this sorrow because greater age brings greater exposure to sin and its consequences. As we pass through time, we see more and more of the sin that lies within our hearts. As we accumulate years of experience, we also accumulate a deeper knowledge of the sin that inhabits other people's hearts and comes out through their words and actions. With every day, with every year, we see and experience in greater measure the consequences of sin in the world around us—death, destruction, disaster. It adds up to a great weight of sorrow.

This sorrow is universal. Even Christians experience sorrow in aging. They, too, find that greater age brings greater sorrow. It comes in many forms. Here are five of them.

THE SORROW OF WEAKNESS

As we age, we experience the sorrow of weakness. Of course, as we first begin to age, we grow stronger. As we pass from infancy into childhood and from childhood into adulthood, our bodies grow and strengthen. From Solomon's vantage point in old age, he says, "Rejoice, O young man, in your youth, and let your heart cheer you in the days of your youth" (Ecclesiastes 11:9a). He goes so far as to say, "The glory of young men is their strength" (Proverbs 20:29).

But that strength does not last long, does it? There are a few years of growth followed by many years of decline, a few years of strength followed by many years of weakness. For men and women alike, physical strength peaks in their 20s or 30s before settling into a long decline. Muscle mass, bone density, metabolism, and even the senses begin to deteriorate. Most athletes retire by 37 or 38 years old, when they still have more than half their lives to live. They simply can't keep up anymore.

> Remember also your Creator in the days of your youth, before the evil days come and the years draw near of which you will say, "I have no pleasure in them"; before the sun and the light and the moon and the stars are darkened and the clouds return after the rain, in the day when the keepers of the house tremble, and the strong men are bent, and the grinders cease because they are few, and those who look through the windows are dimmed, and the doors on the street are shut—when the sound of the grinding is low, and one rises up at the sound of a bird, and all the daughters of song are brought low—they are afraid also of what is high, and terrors are in the way; the almond

tree blossoms, the grasshopper drags itself along, and desire fails... (Ecclesiastes 12:1-5a)

This is a poetic description of the body weakening and failing. Eyes dimming, hands shaking, feet shuffling, back bending, teeth missing, voice trembling. It is a pathetic contrast with the strength and vigor of youth. And the decline of our bodies only grows steeper with age. There is sorrow in seeing our bodies weaken and decay.

THE SORROW OF WEARINESS

Added to the sorrow of weakness is the sorrow of weariness. Old Solomon knew this sorrow as well, for in Ecclesiastes 1:8 he exclaims: "All things are full of weariness; a man cannot utter it; the eye is not satisfied with seeing, nor the ear filled with hearing." A long hike brings deep fatigue; a long life brings deep weariness. How could it do anything else in a world so stained by sin and its consequences? The longer we live, the more of this weariness we experience, and this weariness presses down on our bodies, our minds, our souls.

A pastor once visited my church and told of the trials he and his congregation had been enduring. Most recently and most painfully, his dear friends had lost their unborn child. They had just one opportunity to carry a child and for eight-and-a-half months, and the pregnancy was progressing normally. The day was fast approaching! Then, only two weeks from full-term, the child died and was stillborn. What tragedy. What sorrow. Standing before us that day he said, "I hate this world right now. All it has done is break my heart. None of us want to stay here. All this world does is fool you and fail you. It over-promises and under-delivers." He was expressing the weariness of living in this sinful, painful world—a world of death, destruction, and decay, a world that provides so little purpose and meaning to our suffering. Greater age leads to greater sorrow. It leads to the sorrow of weariness.

THE SORROW OF REAPING

There is also the sorrow of reaping. Reaping is a farming term that refers to gathering a crop. What the farmer plants in spring he harvests in autumn. He reaps what he first sows. Paul warns, "Do not be deceived, God is not mocked; for whatever a man sows, that he will also reap. For he who sows to his flesh will of the flesh reap corruption" (Galatians 6:7-8a). Ultimately and most significantly, this reaping happens after the final judgment when God "will render to each one according to his works" (Romans 2:6). But this reaping begins now, even for believers, for sowing and reaping are spiritual principles in both life and death.

Sowing to the flesh involves pursuing sin as well as failing to pursue good. It involves deepening in depravity as well as failing to grow in righteousness. It involves the natural consequences for our sin. The man who sows adultery reaps a wrecked marriage. He who sows fraud reaps imprisonment. The woman who sows discord reaps loneliness. She who sows self-gratification reaps addiction. On and on it goes. As more life is lived and more sin is sown, more corruption is reaped. Much sin that is sown in youth lies dormant in the soil, until at last it bursts forth and is reaped in old age. The farmer who sows weeds in the spring can't be surprised when the autumn comes and all he has to harvest is weeds. The person who sows a lifetime of sin can't be surprised when the autumn of his life comes and all he has to harvest is sin. "Whatever a man sows, that he will also reap."

THE SORROW OF MORTALITY

Then, compounding all of this sorrow, comes the sorrow of mortality: the knowledge of death's sure approach. As we have already seen, Ecclesiastes 12 speaks of the body's decline, but it also speaks of its inevitable end:

> Man is going to his eternal home, and the mourners go about the streets—before the silver cord is snapped, or the golden bowl is broken, or the pitcher is shattered at the fountain, or the wheel broken at the cistern, and the dust returns to the earth as it was, and the spirit returns to God who gave it. Vanity of vanities, says the Preacher; all is vanity (Ecclesiastes 12:5b-8).

Solomon gives us a picture of a flaxen rope holding a clay pitcher, a means of drawing up nourishment and refreshment. Over time, the rope wears with age and use. Strand by strand, it begins to fray. And then, it succumbs to the inevitable. The rope breaks, and the pitcher plummets to the depths, smashing into pieces. That is the frailty of life and the inevitability of death.

Part of the sorrow of aging is the sorrow of knowing that we are closer to death now than we were before. We are one day closer to death than a day ago, one moment closer to death than a moment ago. That time has passed and we can never have it back. Dreams we had will go unfulfilled, missions we wanted to accomplish will go undone. Friends we've loved have gone on before us, and we feel the pain of their absence. That's the reality of life in this world, a world in which we all pass through time until we come to the end of our time.

THE SORROW OF FEAR

Finally, there is the sorrow of fear. With weakness, weariness, reaping, and the inevitability of death's approach comes fear. It could not be any other way. In Psalm 71, King David voices some of this fear. Looking ahead to old age, he prays, "Do not cast me off in the time of old age; forsake me not when my strength is spent" (Psalm 71:9). He is expressing some of the fear that comes with age, fear that as he gets old he will find himself alone, without an ally, without anyone to care for him through his final days.

As bodies fade and minds diminish, fear increases. Of course it does. This world is scary enough when we are strong and able. How much scarier, then, when we are weak and vulnerable, when we are dependent upon others for our care, our sustenance, our protection. There is a reason so many people prey upon the elderly, which is why the elderly need our special care and protection. Age is fraught with many perils that lead to the sorrow of fear.

FIVE SORROWS, ONE HOPE

Here, then, are five sorrows that come with aging, even to Christians: the sorrow of weakness, the sorrow of weariness, the sorrow of reaping, the sorrow of mortality, and the sorrow of fear. All five of these sorrows would be absent in a perfect, sinless world. All five of them are present and universal in a world like this. All five come with aging and only increase as time goes on.

When we look at aging this way we see that death is the crescendo of a million sorrows. We are dying from the moment we are born. As soon as we begin to move through time, we are moving toward the end of our time.

If these sorrows are inevitable, how can we prepare ourselves? How can we face them well without succumbing to despair, perversion, drunkenness, bitterness, or a hundred other vices? We need to arm ourselves with character that will strengthen and sustain us. We need to embrace the joys and the responsibilities that come with aging. But we can only do this if we first know Christ.

Christ's life began with the very heights of joy, and it ended with sorrows so deep that he is rightly called the Man of Sorrows (Isaiah 53:3). As he lived, he experienced weakness and weariness, fear, and the inevitability of death's approach. And though he was unpolluted by sin, perfect in every thought, word, and deed, still he reaped the fearful consequences of sin—our sin. For on the cross he took our sin upon himself, suffering its full torment, paying its full price. But he rose. He rose! And now he offers forgiveness and life to all who will put their faith in him. Those who believe in Christ have hope that outlasts life and outlasts death. They have the sure hope of resurrection, of life renewed, life restored, life eternal. They are empowered by his grace to endure the sorrows, experience the joys, and embrace the responsibilities that come with aging.

I want to close this chapter with a word of encouragement to those are tempted to despair by what they may reap in old age. Perhaps Christ saved you later in life, after much damage had already been done. Perhaps Christ saved you as a child or teen, but you have since spent many years in apathy or disobedience. You need to know that God's grace is sufficient to redeem your failures. Because of his grace, none of us experience all the negative reaping we should. Because of his grace, none of us have to fear even a moment of this life or the life to come. Yes, there may still be consequences for your sin. But even this will not be purposeless. Even this will be found to have been used by God for his good purposes. Take heart. "Wait for the LORD; be strong, and let your heart take courage; wait for the LORD!" (Psalm 27:14).

CHAPTER 2

Greater Age Brings Greater Joy

We were made to exist within time, to age as we progress through the years allotted to us. We have seen how aging can bring tremendous sorrows—the sorrows of weakness, weariness, reaping, mortality, and fear. But we do not experience only sorrows. We experience joys as well. Some of these extend to believer and unbeliever alike, but God reserves the choicest of his joys for those who live for his glory.

The surging sorrows that come with aging stem from longer exposure to our depravity, to the depravity of others, and to the woeful consequences of sin in this world. The escalating joys stem from longer exposure to God's means of grace, to his Spirit working through his Word, and to his inner work of renewal. Without Christ we cannot know any of these higher joys, but in Christ we can anticipate, experience, and enjoy them all.

In the previous chapter, we looked at five sorrows that come with aging and increase with aging. Now we turn to five joys to see that greater age brings greater joy.

THE JOY OF WISDOM

As we age, we experience the joy of wisdom. One of the Bible's repeated principles is the association of youth with foolishness and of age with wisdom. Job says, "Wisdom is with the aged, and understanding in length of days" (Job 12:12). The purpose of the book of Proverbs is to "give prudence to the simple, knowledge and discretion to the youth," to exhort young people to renounce their in-born folly and embrace wisdom (Proverbs 1:4). This wisdom is far more than a knowledge of how to navigate life and fulfill its responsibilities. True biblical wisdom is putting off the practical atheism that lives within us and putting on the way of thinking that flows from the mind and heart of God. "The fear of the LORD is the beginning of knowledge" (Proverbs 1:7a).

As we age in Christ, we learn more of the Bible, and it takes deeper root in our lives. As the years march on, as we commit ourselves to God's means of grace, the Holy Spirit progressively renews our minds and transforms us from within (Romans 12:1-2). Wisdom is like coffee, not Kool-Aid. We can add a packet of Kool-Aid to water, give it a quick stir, and it is ready. But coffee needs to percolate. To draw out the full flavor, the water needs to pass through the grounds again and again. Wisdom takes time. It takes years of meditation, years of God's Word percolating into our minds, transforming the way we live and think. Wisdom's full flavor is experienced late in life, not early. As we age, we experience the steadily increasing joy of steadily increasing wisdom.

THE JOY OF GODLINESS

Closely connected to the joy of wisdom is the joy of godliness. Proverbs 16:31 says: "Gray hair is a crown of glory; it is gained in a righteous life." Age is associated with godliness, and greater age with greater godliness. Godliness brings nearness to God, relational intimacy with him. "Draw near to God, and he will draw near to you," says James (4:8). The passing of time gives us occasion to read and apply more of God's Word. Each passing year gives more time for the Spirit to impress the truth we've learned on our hearts and continue his inward work of restoration. Each day gives us another opportunity to take hold of the Spirit's power in putting sin to death and coming alive to righteousness. As the years pass, we hear more sermons, we enjoy more Christian fellowship, we participate in the Lord's Supper again and again. God works through it all, through each of these ordinary means, to draw us to closer, deeper relationship with himself. As time marches on, the depraved get more depraved while the godly get more godly.

Paul found joy in this and contrasted a fading body with a surging soul. "Therefore we do not lose heart. Though outwardly we are wasting away, yet inwardly we are being renewed day by day" (2 Corinthians 4:16-18, NIV). What a joy! As Christians, we experience God's day-by-day renewal, and it continues and increases as we age. Financial interest compounds, so that small, steady deposits over a lifetime lead to the wealth needed for a comfortable retirement. Godliness also compounds, so that small, steady gains over sin and small, steady acts of righteousness lead to a great treasury of godliness in old age. As we look to the future, we will be godlier than we are today, godlier than we ever dared imagine. We continue to become like Christ until the day we see the face of Christ.

THE JOY OF RESPECT

With aging we also experience the joy of respect, the right to be respected by those who are younger. Leviticus 19:32 lays out this principle: "You shall stand up before the gray head and honor the face of an old man." The Bible demands that the young give honor and respect to the elderly. Respect for the aged is closely aligned with respect for God, since God has ordained that the old should lead the young, that their wisdom should influence and restrain youthful folly.

This respect is not meant to be displayed only in words and attitudes ("honor the face of an old man"), but also in actions ("stand up before the gray head"). The young are to take an interest in the elderly, to assist them, visit them, include them, befriend them, seek them for their wisdom. Even while contemporary Western culture disparages age and celebrates youth, young Christians are to honor the old. The old are to accept the honor and to embrace both the privilege and the responsibility that comes with it. Those who have attained years are worthy of honor. Those who have attained wisdom and godliness through the years are worthy of double honor.

THE JOY OF REAPING

Then there is the joy of reaping. We have already looked at Paul's words in Galatians to see that those who live a corrupt life will reap the ugly consequences, even on this side of the grave. There is sorrow in reaping, but there is joy, too. "Do not be deceived: God is not mocked, for whatever one sows, that will he also reap. For the one who sows to his flesh will from the flesh reap corruption, *but the one who sows to the Spirit will from the Spirit reap eternal life*" (Galatians 6:7-8). Even in this life, we get to experience the benefits of living to the glory of God. This is the wisdom, the respect, and the godliness that come with aging in Christ. Those who sow good seed begin to harvest even now, and to harvest in greater measure as life goes by. But there's more.

As we age, we begin to experience new joys, joys that we cannot experience apart from aging. Some reap the precious harvest of children and grandchildren who know and love the Lord. Proverbs 17:6 declares, "Children's children are a crown to the aged" (NIV). Some reap the reward of faithful service. When Paul writes to Timothy to discuss the proper ordering of the local church, he instructs him to honor widows who have served the church well, to care for them as a return for all the ways they cared for others (1 Timothy 5:1-16). The same is expected of children toward their parents—"But if a widow has children or grandchildren, let them first learn to show godliness to their own household and to make some return to their parents, for this is pleasing in the sight of God" (1 Timothy 5:4). As we progress in life, we begin to experience the beautiful consequences of a life lived in God's way to God's glory.

THE JOY OF MORTALITY

Then, finally, there is the joy of mortality. We know that death's approach brings sorrow, but it also brings joy. We might think of Simeon, the old man who met baby Jesus at the temple. "He took him up in his arms and blessed God and said, 'Lord, now you are letting your servant depart in peace, according to your word; for my eyes have seen your salvation'" (Luke 2:28-30). After a lifetime of serving God, dear old Simeon could depart in peace and confidence because he had seen Christ. He knew his Savior, he looked forward to death, he looked forward to eternal peace, eternal reward.

The Apostle Paul regarded death as joy, not sorrow. "For to me to live is Christ, and to die is gain" (Philippians 1:21). In fact, he was eager to die ("My desire is to depart and be with Christ, for that is far better"), though he was also willing to remain to serve God's people ("But to remain in the flesh is more necessary on your account"). With the confidence of knowing Christ, he could proclaim: "'Death is swallowed up in victory.' 'O death, where is your victory? O death, where is your sting?'"

Aging brings greater awareness of death's inevitable

approach. But for the Christian, death has lost its sting, its terror. Death is the gateway to being more alive than we have ever been, the doorway to Christ himself. Every day we age in Christ, we grow one day closer to seeing Christ, to embracing Christ, to enjoying his presence forever. What joy!

FIVE JOYS

Aging is associated with sorrows, but it is also associated with joys. The Bible promises that for those who age in Christ, there are benefits stored up in this life and the life to come. There is the joy of wisdom, of godliness, of respect, of reaping, and of mortality. God is faithful to provide what he has promised.

As we age, our physical strength will diminish. Yet even as physical strength fails, spiritual strength surges. Time, the enemy of the body, is a friend to the soul. When we are young we are physically strong and spiritually weak, but when we are old we are spiritually strong and physically weak. With so great a reward ahead, the challenge is clear: if we are to live the most meaningful lives, lives that glorify God, we must age in Christ. Aging in Christ will not remove all of the sorrows, but it will add the joys.

As we continue, we need to ask these questions: How do we deal well with the inevitable sorrows, so that they do not drive us to bitterness, drunkenness, or the other foul vices that overtake so many as they age? How can we experience the fullness of these joys? We combat the sorrows and enhance the joys by embracing the God-given responsibilities that come with greater age and putting on more and more of the character he commends.

CHAPTER 3

The Race

This booklet began with the word picture of a prison or palace. I asked what kind of home you are preparing for yourself as you grow older—a place of sorrowful captivity or a place of joyful comfort. I borrowed this metaphor from a favorite writer of days gone by. Now I'd like to introduce a second metaphor drawn straight from the Bible: life as an athletic event.

As Paul wrote to the church in Corinth, he said,

> Do you not know that in a race all the runners run, but only one receives the prize? So run that you may obtain it. Every athlete exercises self-control in all things. They do it to receive a perishable wreath, but we an imperishable. So I do not run aimlessly; I do not box as one beating the air. But I discipline my body and keep it under control, lest after preaching to others I myself should be disqualified (1 Corinthians 9:24–27).

Just as a tennis metaphor might resonate with a congregation near Wimbledon, this athletic metaphor resonated with the church in Corinth. Since Corinth was the location of the biannual Isthmian games, every Corinthian was familiar with the events and their grueling training regimens. Here Paul describes runners and boxers, both of whom train relentlessly so they can perform to the highest standards and win the great prize. The author of Hebrews uses a similar running metaphor when he says, "Therefore, since we are surrounded by so great a cloud of witnesses, let us also lay aside every weight, and sin which clings so closely, and let us run with endurance the race that is set before us, looking to Jesus..." (Hebrews 12:1-2).

Life is a race that demands the highest standards of preparation. It demands carefully planned strategies, deep reserves of stamina, and an overwhelming desire to break the tape in victory. Yet this race is different from any other in that we do not compete against one another, but against ourselves and the great enemies of every Christian: the world, the flesh, and the devil. Those who do not prepare for such obstacles and who do not overcome them will not finish the race, but instead be shamefully disqualified.

Paul was convinced he had run this race well, for by the end of his life he told Timothy, "I have fought the good fight, I have finished the race, I have kept the faith. Henceforth there is laid up for me the crown of righteousness, which the Lord, the righteous judge, will award to me on that day, and not only to me but also to all who have loved his appearing" (2 Timothy 4:7-8). We have this kind of athletic mindset in so many other areas of life: our careers, our health, our hobbies. And yet, many of us think that godly aging is a stroll in the park, something that will simply "happen" with the passing of time. Paul is telling us here that godliness comes only with planning and great effort. It requires the same level of diligence and discipline that athletes bring to their training. How are you doing in this great fight, this great competition?

Right now you are running your race. Only God knows whether the finish line is nearby or far off in the distance. But whether it is near or far, you bear the responsibility of running well, of running in such a way that you will finish the race in victory.

CHAPTER 4

Greater Age Brings Greater Responsibility

Aging is a universal reality in this world, for as time progresses, we progress with it. Aging brings many sorrows as we face greater exposure to the sin that lives within us and the sin that pollutes everything around us. Aging also brings many joys as we experience God's rich blessings, and especially as we receive greater exposure to his renewing work. If sorrows are inevitable, is there a way of living that can diminish their impact? Is there something we can do so that these sorrows do not drive us to bitterness, vice, or despair? And if joys are possible, is there a way of living that allows us to experience more of them, to experience them in their fullness?

One of the ways to diminish the sorrows and amplify the joys is to embrace the responsibility that comes with aging. Throughout the Bible, God associates aging with responsibility. With increased age comes increased responsibility. Here are five of the responsibilities that come with age and increase with age.

THE RESPONSIBILITY OF MATURITY

With aging comes the responsibility of maturity. No matter our age, it's our responsibility to act that age. No matter how old we are or how long we have been Christians, we need to grow up and keep growing up. We see the connection between time and maturity in many places in the New Testament, but particularly in the letter to the Hebrews, where a concerned pastor challenges his church in this area. "About this we have much to say, and it is hard to explain, since you have become dull of hearing. For though by this time you ought to be teachers, you need someone to teach you again the basic principles of the oracles of God. You need milk, not solid food" (Hebrews 5:11-12). He reminds his congregation that much time has passed since they came to a saving knowledge of Jesus Christ. That time has given them opportunity to mature, but they haven't. While their physical age has increased, their spiritual maturity has actually decreased. He warns them: You need to grow up! You need to act your spiritual age! Of course, there are many who become Christians later in life, which will affect their level of spiritual maturity in old age. But the fact remains that older men and older women who are older Christians carry the responsibility of spiritual maturity.

To our growing maturity we need to add humility, so that we do not act above our station, overstepping the boundaries of our years. Where we have not yet gained authority we must not speak as if we have. The man who has been married for two years has no business speaking as if he has been married for twenty. The woman whose oldest child is a toddler must guard herself from speaking as if she has already successfully raised her children to independence. Paul warns Timothy, "Do not rebuke an older man but encourage him as you would a father..." (1 Timothy 5:1a). Young Timothy had no business castigating an older man. If he had to exhort an older man living in sin, he was to do it with respect and humility.

As we age, we gain the responsibility to act in a way fitting for that age. This is true of our physical age and our spiritual age. We need to grow up!

THE RESPONSIBILITY OF INVOLVEMENT

Added to this is the responsibility of involvement, and especially involvement in the local church. When we are young, it can be easy and exciting to be deeply engaged in a church community. But as we reach adulthood and continue to age, life has a way of interfering even with something as valuable as church. The duties of life threaten to push us away from our friendships, our service, and even our worship. Education, work, children, grandchildren, and hobbies are all tremendous blessings, but even they can diminish our investment and involvement in the church. Or perhaps the burdens of aging and the compounding sorrows of life can cause us to be withdrawn.

We do well listen to David's praise and prayer in Psalm 71: "O God, from my youth you have taught me, and I still proclaim your wondrous deeds. So even to old age and gray hairs, O God, do not forsake me, until I proclaim your might to another generation, your power to all those to come" (17-18).

Even in old age, even with gray hair, David knew it was his responsibility to proclaim God's power to the next generation. The wisdom and godliness represented by his gray head were exactly what the next generation needed. His years had allowed him to accumulate great storehouses of wisdom, maturity, humility—what was so desperately lacking in his children and children's children. David determined that he would never use his age as an excuse. He understood that with increased age came heightened responsibility. He would stay involved, he would remain invested, to the glory of God.

THE RESPONSIBILITY OF EXAMPLE

Then there is the responsibility of example, of setting an example of the character and conduct that God commends. We expect little from children when it comes to modeling such traits. But as they grow into their teens and then pass into their 20s and 30s, we rightly expect much more. With aging we gain the special responsibility of setting an example to those who are younger than we are. Titus 2:2-3 lays out specific ways that older people are to serve as an example to younger people. "Older men are to be sober-minded, dignified, self-controlled, sound in faith, in love, and in steadfastness. Older women likewise are to be reverent in behavior, not slanderers or slaves to much wine. They are to teach what is good..." Older men are to cultivate and display specific character traits—traits that are appropriate for their age and lacking in those who are younger. Older women, too, gain new responsibilities of character and conduct that serve as an example to younger women.

No matter our age, we are responsible to set an example to others, and especially to those who are younger than we are. In God's design, we tend to look at people who are just a little bit further along. We admire them, we imitate them, we want to be like them. For that reason, we all must display the character and conduct that serve as a fitting example for those who will soon be our physical and spiritual age. The more we age, the more we grow into this special responsibility.

THE RESPONSIBILITY OF MENTORING

Closely related to the responsibility of example is the responsibility of mentoring. It is not enough merely to set an example. We also need to take an interest in people who are younger than we are, to be involved in their lives, and to deliberately teach and train them. The passage in Titus 2 continues in this way: "Older women ... are to teach what is good, and so train the young women to love their husbands and children, to be self-controlled, pure, working at home, kind, and submissive to their own husbands, that the word of God may not be reviled. Likewise, urge the younger men to be self-controlled" (3-6).

By virtue of their age, along with wisdom and godliness that attend it, older women gain the responsibility of teaching and training younger women. They are to teach these younger women to exercise wisdom, to display godliness, and in turn, to set an example to the generation that will follow them. Older men gain the same responsibility toward younger men.

It is as if the mature Christian has been climbing a trail up a long, steep mountain. Some stretches have taken every bit of effort and every bit of skill to navigate safely. He has almost reached the summit but turns to see a friend coming up behind. This friend has made good progress, but he has come to a part of the trail that is especially dangerous. What is our leader to do? He is to help, of course. Though he may not have the strength to carry his young friend up the mountain, he has the experience to demonstrate and the wisdom to guide. As we age, each of us becomes responsible for those who are aging behind us.

THE RESPONSIBILITY OF WATCHFULNESS

One further responsibility that comes with aging and increases with greater aging is the responsibility of watchfulness. We tend to associate falling into sin with youth, with the desire for wanton pleasure that marks so many young people. We read the alarming statistics about how many young people drift away from their parents' religion as soon as they gain their independence. Yet greater age only heightens the need for watchfulness, for as Paul warns, "Therefore let anyone who thinks that he stands take heed lest he fall" (1 Corinthians 10:12).

There are some, perhaps many, who fall away in old age. We can think of young Solomon, who showed such promise and displayed such wisdom. Yet "when Solomon was old his wives turned away his heart after other gods, and his heart was not wholly true to the LORD his God, as was the heart of David his father" (1 Kings 11:4). Solomon was swayed by lifelong patterns of foolish disobedience. He failed to keep watch and very nearly made shipwreck of his faith. It was only the grace of God that held off the fearsome consequences of Solomon's sin.

There are many who profess faith in Christ in their youth and fall away before the end. Some fall in their early years, some in the middle, many near the end. These are the ones who fail to embrace and maintain the responsibility of watchfulness.

FIVE RESPONSIBILITIES

Here we have five responsibilities that come to us by virtue of aging—the responsibilities of maturity, involvement, example, mentoring, and watchfulness. Embracing these responsibilities helps diminish the sorrows that come to all who live in this world. It helps enhance the fullness of the joys that come with aging. It ensures that our gray hairs will be a crown of glory rather than a crown of shame (Proverbs 16:31).

CHAPTER 5

The Fruitful Tree

We are now going to add a third metaphor to our collection: the metaphor of a fruitful tree. David spoke of this in Psalm 92, a song of hope and confidence.

> The righteous flourish like the palm tree and grow like a cedar in Lebanon. They are planted in the house of the LORD; they flourish in the courts of our God. They still bear fruit in old age; they are ever full of sap and green, to declare that the LORD is upright; he is my rock, and there is no unrighteousness in him. (Psalm 92:12-15)

Here David looks to days still to come and declares his confidence that even in old age God will see him, love him, and uphold him. He compares himself and all believers to the great palm tree that bears fruit and to the massive cedar that surpasses all others in its grandeur and strength. Where the wicked will perish and be scattered, the righteous will flourish and remain. Even in old age, they will know God because they are known by God. Even to their final breath, they will declare the greatness of their King. Their last days will be their most fruitful days, the due reward of a life lived to his glory.

What is it that causes these trees to flourish? It is their nearness to God. "They are planted in the house of the LORD; they flourish in the courts of our God." These, like the trees of Psalm 1, are nourished by God to remain strong forever. We can only age well when we age near God.

GREATER AGE BRINGS GOOD GIFTS

When Aileen and I were young and almost married, there was one old couple in the church whom we grew to love and respect above all others. Mr. and Mrs. Lubberts were a dear old couple who had lived in Holland through the Second World War and the German occupation and, like so many of their countrymen, had immigrated to Canada after the war drew to its close. There were two qualities we especially admired: their great godliness and their deep and lasting love for one another. They were full of joy and full of godliness. We looked up to this couple and loved to spend time with them. One of my enduring memories is seeing them pull up outside the church in their great big car and walking into the church hand-in-hand, still in love after 60 years of marriage.

Aileen and I wanted to be like the Lubbertses. We still do. We want to be godly like they were godly and be in love like they were in love, even in old age. The Lord gives us these models of godly old age so we can see, admire, and imitate them. They model how to age well by enjoying the good gifts that God brings with aging.

The book of Ecclesiastes is invaluable for those who desire to live a godly old age. It provides invaluable wisdom for how to relate to the things of the world. The author calls himself the "Preacher," but from what he tells about himself and what history has recorded of him, we are confident that he is king Solomon. This is the great and wise and powerful king near the end of his life. He puts aside his kingly crown to speak as the sage, as the Preacher. This is not the young man, the temple-builder, the man who romances his lover in Song of Solomon. By this time, Solomon had accumulated more wealth, more possessions, and more power than any of us could imagine. He understood how the things of the world can rob our joy. But he also knew best how to enjoy the gifts of God. This is the old and wise man who tells us, "This is how God wants you to live your lives. From my perspective here in old age, I can now see what life is all about."

I don't think any passage in Scripture has shaped my life to a greater extent than Ecclesiastes 11:7 to 12:8. I heard it preached when I was a teen, and it has resonated in my mind and heart ever since. It has challenged me to acknowledge this: Those who want to be joyful in old age must learn to be joyful now. And in order to be joyful now, we must learn how to enjoy God's good gifts.

THREE WAYS TO ENJOY LIFE

The Preacher truly wants us to be joyful. He wants us to live life to the full. He wants us to delight in the good things of this world and the good things that life brings. He wants us to appreciate the beauty in a sunset, he wants us to savor a delicious meal, he wants us to linger over a great cup of coffee, he wants us to look long and deep in the eyes of the person we love, he wants us to delight in the crack of a bat hitting a ball. All of this is good and honoring to God. He made this world and all that is delightful in it, and he wants us to enjoy it. We give glory to God when we delight in his good gifts.

In all these commands to enjoy life, the Preacher gives us three joy-enhancers, three ways of helping us find the truest pleasures and the greatest joys.

First, *enjoy life, but acknowledge that youth will end.* He says, "If a person lives many years, let him rejoice in them all; but let him remember that the days of darkness will be many" (11:8). We are to savor life as we live it. If we are granted many years, we are free before the Lord to live them all without sadness and without regret. This is good and glorious. But even as we take joy in life, even as we live with youthful exuberance, our Preacher calls us to have an awareness that the light of day will eventually give way to the dark of night. The sun that rises will need to set again and darkness will come. The joy of youth will be followed by all the difficulties of old age and the difficulties of old age will be followed by death. It is right and good to live to the fullest. But we live best when we keep one eye on eternity, when we keep in mind that these good days will come to an end.

Acknowledging the end helps us. It reinforces that we only get one chance, one opportunity. This life cannot be lived well in retrospect, but only in the moment. We will not be given a second chance to do life well. We will not be given a second chance to do today well. We must live it all with joy.

Second, *enjoy life but acknowledge a coming judgment.* "Walk in the ways of your heart and the sight of your eyes. But know that for all these things God will bring you into judgment" (11:9). We might think that it's too risky for our Preacher to call a young man to live according to the ways of his heart and the light of his eyes. This could easily be seen as a call to hedonism, to live only for the pleasure of this life. But it's not this simple. Our joy in life is to be an innocent joy, a pure and moral and ethical joy. If we look elsewhere in Ecclesiastes, elsewhere in the Bible, we find that God gives us boundaries and tells us to live within them. Why? Because he made us, and he knows that the greatest pleasures are found within those boundaries, not outside of them. God cares for our joy so much that he tells us what to avoid and what to pursue in order to find the highest joy. These days of youth and all of their pleasures are lived out before God, who will weigh and assess each one of them.

Third, *enjoy life but acknowledge the vanity of it.* Twice the Preacher tells us that life is vanity. "All is vanity" and "youth and the dawn of life are vanity" (11:10). The ESV translates this word from the Hebrew as "vanity," but another acceptable translation is "vapor." All that comes between life and death is vapor. It isn't quite meaningless and it isn't quite futile, but it is vapor, something that is here today and gone tomorrow, like dust blown away by the wind.

What we do in this life matters. It has significance. But nothing here will ultimately satisfy because nothing here will last forever. Earlier in Ecclesiastes the Preacher says that God has put eternity in our hearts. How could anything less than eternity give us ultimate satisfaction? True, there are good things in the world. But we were made for more than anything this world can provide.

This is a warning for us. It is a warning that we are surrounded by false joys. Fraudulent joys. Things that try to convince us that they will satisfy, but they will only leave us empty. Really, this is a warning that we will always be tempted to be idolaters, to turn the gift into the god.

If we want to enjoy the fullest pleasures of food, we must enjoy it in moderation, not in gluttony. We must enjoy it as a gift, not as a god that controls us. If we want to enjoy the highest joys of sex, we must rejoice in the husband or wife God provides and find satisfaction only in him or her. Every joy in this life is meant to point beyond itself to the one who allows us to experience such joy and such pleasure.

Before he moves on, the Preacher gives one more command on how to live this way. "Remove vexation from your heart, and put away pain from your body" (11:10). He commands us to put away whatever it is that is hindering us from fully enjoying life. Don't be depressed. Don't be sad. Don't be bitter. Don't miss the beauty of the sunrise because we know that eventually there will be a sunset. Don't let these good gifts spoil without enjoying them.

Live. Really live! While we are alive, while we have energy and enthusiasm and ability, live a full and enjoyable life. Pursue pleasure, pursue passions. This is a limited time, but a beautiful time, meant to be fully enjoyed. Youth is a gift from God, and he wants us to accept and treasure his gift. These good and exciting and youthful days are preparing us for what will come. They are a training ground. They are where we set the trajectory of character that will take us into and then through the dark days that will come.

God wants us to rejoice. We should never feel ashamed for enjoying a morning cup of coffee with the wife of our youth. We shouldn't try to hide the heart-felt happiness that comes with a beautifully composed song or a spellbinding movie. These gifts are made for our enjoyment. But even more than that, they are made to point us to the giver. So enjoy life, but know that death is approaching. Enjoy life, but keep your eyes on the coming judgment. Enjoy life, but set your hope on God rather than the vapor of his gifts.

Why do we love people like the Lubbertses? We love them because they were joyful and godly in old age. From a young age, they knew how to enjoy the good gift of marriage, even while they pursued godliness. And that joy and that godliness sustained them through even the darkest days of old age. We see that. We love that. We want that. And with God's grace and by obeying God's Word, we can have it

CHAPTER 6

Greater Age Brings Life-Shaping Decisions

I remember watching the commercial as a child. A man dressed for office work sprints after a bus, desperate to flag it down before it drives off without him. In a flash, he finds himself on a beach where he sees his future self, jogging in the morning sun. His future self looks over and asks, "Still in the rat race?" "Hey, you're me!," he replies. His future self is retired, healthy, free. "Retirement agrees with me." "Retirement? How can we afford that?" The answer? "Freedom 55."

Freedom 55, a financial-planning company, held out an attractive promise: labor for 30 years, retire at 55, and enjoy a long, comfortable retirement. But it also held out an entire philosophy of life: true freedom is found in leisure. The good life is the free life—free from children, expectation, vocation. Many live with this as their motivation, their destination, their heaven on earth. The Bible holds out something better—something far more challenging but far more satisfying.

Paul, the seasoned veteran, writes to young Timothy, "Train yourself for godliness; for while bodily training is of some value, godliness is of value in every way, as it holds promise for the present life and also for the life to come" (1 Timothy 4:7b-8). Godliness is the goal of every Christian's life because it alone holds promise for this life and for the life to come. In some mysterious but sure way, the godliness we achieve in this life carries over to eternity. That is a promise no retirement plan can match. The retirement dream accounts for this life, but it gives us nothing when death comes. It stores up enough treasure for a carefree retirement, but it leaves us destitute for what follows. Only godliness accumulates treasure in an account that can't be touched by death. The philosophy of Freedom 55 is worldliness, a way of thinking that is detached from the wisdom of God.

Godliness is to be our desire and our aim from the moment of conversion to the moment of death. All the while, worldliness will be our temptation. No matter our age, no matter how far we have traveled through time, we are to relentlessly pursue godliness and persistently avoid worldliness. Just as an athlete disciplines his body and mind, just as he dedicates himself to the pursuit of excellence, we Christians must apply discipline and dedication to our pursuit of godliness. We must train ourselves and push ourselves until we have completed our race. If we ever slow our pursuit of godliness, now or in old age, we deny the connection between now and forever. We deny the resurrection.

As we train ourselves in godliness, we will inevitably encounter temptations custom-crafted to each stage of life. Worldliness will manifest itself in different ways and we will have to make choices. Here in the final chapter, I mean to share wisdom to help us avoid the worldly temptations that come with aging. I haven't run far enough in my race to have this wisdom, so I read a half-dozen books written by seasoned runners, by Christians who write from the perspective of old age. As I read I asked, *What are the choices we will have to make as we age? What choices will lead us to age well? What decisions do we need to make right now?* Here is what I learned.[2]

CHOOSE ZEAL OVER APATHY

As we age, we face a growing temptation toward apathy. When we are young we are zealous, easily enthused by ideas, desires, and causes. We have energy and enthusiasm in abundance. But as we age, as we accumulate responsibilities and experience sorrows, we may face growing apathy and waning passion for God. Romans 12:11 offers a life-long, all-consuming challenge: "Do not be slothful in zeal, be fervent in spirit, serve the Lord." In the words of J.C. Ryle, zeal is "a burning desire to please God, to do his will, to advance his glory in the world in every possible way."[3] It is single-minded devotion to God.

Zeal in old age begins with zeal today, for zeal stirs up a great fire that will never burn out. It generates the enthusiasm for the Lord that will sustain us through what Solomon refers to as the many "days of darkness" to come (Ecclesiastes 11:8). J.I. Packer says, "The challenge that faces us is not to let [declining health] slow us down spiritually, but to cultivate the maximum zeal for the closing phase of our earthly lives."[4] Complacency in our younger days will lead to apathy in our older days. Far better, spiritual enthusiasm in our younger days will promote zeal to the very end. The final leg of our race ought to be a full-out sprint in our pursuit of godliness. Piper offers this challenge: "Knowing that we have an infinitely satisfying and everlasting inheritance in God just over the horizon of life makes us zealous in our few remaining years here to spend ourselves in the sacrifices of love, not the accumulation of comforts."[5] Zeal in our later days begins with zeal in our earlier days. Choose zeal today.

CHOOSE DISCIPLINE OVER COMPLACENCY

If apathy and zeal speak to motivation, complacency and discipline speak to action. Specifically, they speak to the action of putting sin to death and coming alive to righteousness. In 1 Corinthians 9:24-27, Paul turns to the metaphor of a race and warns of the high cost of inaction:

> Do you not know that in a race all the runners run, but only one receives the prize? So run that you may obtain it. Every athlete exercises self-control in all things. They do it to receive a perishable wreath, but we an imperishable. So I do not run aimlessly; I do not box as one beating the air. But I discipline my body and keep it under control, lest after preaching to others I myself should be disqualified."

Paul fought complacency and pursued self-discipline so that no sin would take root in his life and leave him ashamed.

The more we age, the more we need to resist complacency and, instead, discipline ourselves to put off sin and put on righteousness. We need to discipline our *bodies* to ensure we behave with self-control rather than lust. We need to discipline our *minds* to ensure we do not welcome evil thoughts. We need to discipline our *imaginations* to ensure we delight in what is good and refuse to fantasize about what God forbids. We need to discipline our *mouths* to ensure we only speak words that build up. We need to discipline our *time* to ensure we put every moment to effective use. In every way, we must be disciplined in our pursuit of God, building habits of holiness. We must not succumb to the ease of complacency.

CHOOSE LEARNING OVER STAGNATION

A further temptation of aging is the temptation to stagnation, especially in regard to learning. Young people lack knowledge and wisdom, so their younger years are filled with learning. But as we age, we may come to believe we have learned enough to carry us to the end. Yet the Christian life is one of constant mind-renewal that depends upon accumulating the knowledge of God as contained in the Word of God. Until our minds have been completely purged of sin and filled with righteousness, we must continue to learn. "Do not be conformed to this world, but be transformed by the renewal of your mind, that by testing you may discern what is the will of God, what is good and acceptable and perfect" (Romans 12:2).

The full and final transformation of our minds will come only in the presence of Christ. Until then, there is still sin to cleanse, wisdom to apply, truth to enjoy. Donald and George Sweeting point out that a characteristic of those who finish well is that they have a teachable spirit through life. "'Teachable' means that they maintain a humble posture and are open to receiving midcourse corrections. Those who finish well never stop doing this. They are lifelong learners. They learn from reading, from watching and listening to others, and from life itself. This keeps them from plateauing." [6]

We learn not only for our own sanctification, but also for others' benefit. When we share what we have learned with those around us, they are also built up in the faith. We cannot stop learning when there is still truth to teach. "Remember the days of old; consider the years of many generations; ask your father, and he will show you, your elders, and they will tell you" (Deuteronomy 32:7). What we have learned we must pass on. We must become learners now so that we will not slacken our pursuit of learning in our final days.

CHOOSE INVOLVEMENT OVER ISOLATION

We must also resist the temptation of isolation, and especially isolation from church community. Instead, we must pursue and maintain church involvement as long as we are able and as much as we are able. In the midst of a society that honors youth and disparages age, we have God's assurance that age gives us wisdom. And we also have God's charge to bless others with that wisdom. There is a place for people of all ages in the local church. When Paul wrote to the congregation in Philippi, he addressed young and old alike when he said, "Only let your manner of life be worthy of the gospel of Christ, so that whether I come and see you or am absent, I may hear of you that you are standing firm in one spirit, with one mind striving side by side for the faith of the gospel" (Philippians 1:27). In the community of Christians, we stand together as we resist the onslaught of the devil. The young need the old just as the old need the young.

Since God does not revoke our gifts in old age, he does not negate our responsibility to use them for the benefit of others. Perhaps Paul had an awareness of the temptation to isolation when he wrote, "And let us not grow weary of doing good, for in due season we will reap, if we do not give up" (Galatians 6:9). Of course we may have to slow down in our service or hand off our ministries. Instead of the public ministry of preaching, we may have to give ourselves to the quiet ministry of prayer. But to withdraw from Christian service altogether or to cease using the Spirit's gifting is pure disobedience. Speaking to elderly Christians, Packer warns that spiritual gifts don't wither with age, they atrophy with disuse.[7] We need to exercise our gifts when we are young and continue to exercise them the best we can for as long as we can.

CHOOSE HOPE OVER DESPAIR

Finally, as we age we will experience the temptation to despair, the temptation to give up. We guard ourselves by pursuing hope. In Paul's second letter to the Corinthians, he is aware of his increasing age and decreasing health. He knows his "outer self is wasting away" (2 Corinthians 4:16b), yet he remains confident and unbroken. He is convinced he will not lose heart (16a). Packer shows how Paul grounds this hope in four great truths: He has a perfected body awaiting him beyond the grave (5:1); this perfected body will come to him in a perfected place that is far better (5:3-5); when he receives this body he will be at home with Christ (5:6-9); and he will be judged faithful by Christ and, by grace, receive a fitting reward (5:10-11). He is armed with truth and this truth gives him hope—hope enough to sustain him through all pain, all trauma, all temptation to despair. "It was always [God's] plan," says Packer, "that we, his embodied rational creatures, should live our lives in this world looking forward to, and preparing for, something even better than we have known already."[8]

As Christians, we can be confident we have been "born again to a living hope through the resurrection of Jesus Christ from the dead, to an inheritance that is imperishable, undefiled, and unfading, kept in heaven for you, who by God's power are being guarded through faith for a salvation ready to be revealed in the last time" (1 Peter 1:3-5). Our hope is a living hope because we serve a living Savior. And this Savior is guarding us through faith, keeping us from stumbling just as he is keeping our eternal inheritance from fading. Until then, we find hope in the God who promised Isaiah, "Even to your old age and gray hairs I am he, I am he who will sustain you. I have made you and I will carry you; I will sustain you and I will rescue you" (Isaiah 46:4). Even to old age.

CONCLUSION

We are all aging. We are passing through time until we reach the end of our time. We find that greater age brings greater sorrow, but that it also brings greater joy, especially to those who are in Christ. God tells us that greater age brings greater responsibility and that at every age we will need to flee the temptation of worldliness, choosing instead to do what honors and glorifies him. To age gracefully, we must age in Christ and for Christ.

NOTES

1　This section was inspired by "Beautiful Old Age" in *Week-day Religion* by J.R. Miller. The book is no longer in print but can be found in various electronic formats.

2　Books include: *Rethinking Retirement* by John Piper; *Finishing Our Course with Joy* by J.I. Packer; *Finishing Well to the Glory of God* by John Dunlop; *How To Finish the Christian Life* by Donald & George Sweeting; *God Took Me By the Hand* by Jerry Bridges.

3　J.C. Ryle, *Christian Zeal.*

4　J.I. Packer, *Finishing Our Course With Joy.*

5　John Piper, *Rethinking Retirement.*

6　Donald & George Sweeting, *How to Finish the Christian Life.*

7　Packer.

8　Packer.

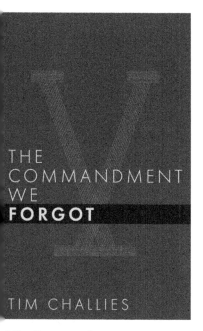

The Commandment We Forgot
Tim Challies

The fifth commandment—"Honor your father and your mother"—is not just for children. Rather, it pertains to the whole of life and to every person of every age. In the home, the church, and the workplace, it provides a stable foundation for all of society. Yet we often neglect it and fail to appreciate its relevance to our lives. It is the commandment we forgot.

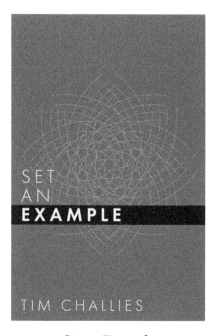

Set an Example
Tim Challies

There are many ways to invest your time in your teens and 20's, but the Bible is clear: none is better than the pursuit of godliness. In Paul's letter to young Timothy, you (yes, you!) are called to be an example to your peers and even to older Christians. He calls you to set an example of maturity and godliness in your speech, conduct, love, faith, and purity.

The Scars That Have Shaped Me
How God Meets Us in Suffering

by Vaneethat Rendall Risner
Foreword by Joni Eareckson Tada

"Raw, transparent, terrifiying, and yet amazingly hopeful!"
Brian Fikkert, co-author of *When Helping Hurts*

Published for Desiring God by Cruciform Press

"Vaneetha writes with creativity, biblical faithfulness, compelling style, and an experiential authenticity that draws other sufferers in. Here you will find both a tested life and a love for the sovereignty of a good and gracious God."
John Piper, author of* Desiring God *and many other books

"*The Scars That Have Shaped Me* will make you weep and rejoice not just because it brims with authenticity and integrity, but because every page points you to the rest that is found in entrusting your life to one who is in complete control and is righteous, powerful, wise, and good in every way."
Paul Tripp, pastor, author, international conference speaker

""I could not put this book down, except to wipe my tears. Vaneetha's testimony of God's kindness to her in pain was exactly what I needed; no doubt, many others will feel the same. It has helped me process my own grief and loss, and given me renewed hope to care for those in my life who suffer in various ways."
***Gloria Furman, author,* Missional Motherhood; Alive in Him**

"Vaneetha Risner's credibility makes us willing to lean in and listen. Her writing is built on her experience of deep pain, and in the midst of that her rugged determination to hold on to Christ."
***Nancy Guthrie, author,* Hearing Jesus Speak into Your Sorrow**

Grieving, Hope and Solace
When a Loved One Dies in Christ

by Albert N. Martin

There is comfort for the grief. There are answers to the questions. The Bible does offer hope, solace, healing, and confidence.

Pastor Albert Martin has been there.

"This tender book by a much-loved pastor, written after the death of his beloved wife, offers comfort to those in tears. A rare guidebook to teach us how to grieve with godliness, it is relevant to us all – if not for today, then no doubt for tomorrow."
Maurice Roberts, former editor, **Banner of Truth** *magazine*

"Albert N. Martin is a seasoned pastor, skilled teacher, and gifted writer who has given us a priceless treasure in this book. All who read these pages will, unquestionably, be pointed to Christ and find themselves greatly helped."
Steve Lawson, Christ Fellowship Baptist Church, Mobile, AL

"Like turning the corner and being met by a glorious moonrise, or discovering a painter or musician who touches us in the deepest recesses of our being—this little book by Pastor Al Martin has been such an experience for me. Whether you are a pastor or counselor, one who is experiencing the pangs of grief, or a member of the church who wants to be useful to others, you need to read this book."
Joseph Pipa, President, Greenville Presbyterian Theo. Sem.

"Personal tenderness and biblical teaching in a sweet book of comfort. Buy it and give it away, but make sure to get a copy for yourself."
Dr. Joel R. Beeke, President, Puritan Reformed Theo. Sem.

Inductive Bible Studies for Women by Keri Folmar

Endorsed by Kathleen Nielson, Diane Schreiner,
Connie Dever, Kristie Anyabwile, Gloria Furman

JOY! – A Bible Study
on Philippians
for Women
A 10-week study

GRACE: A Bible
Study on Ephesians
for Women
A 10-week study

FAITH: A Bible
Study on James
for Women
A 10-week study

A Bible Study for Women on the Gospel of Mark

SON OF GOD
Volume 1
An 11-week study

SON OF GOD
Volume 2
An 11-week study

"It is hard to imagine a better inductive Bible Study tool."
–Diane Schreiner

Made in United States
Orlando, FL
08 May 2022

17659412R00029